Buddy's Blue Day

by

R.A. Berry

AuthorHouse™
1663 Liberty Drive
Bloomington, IN 47403
www.authorhouse.com
Phone: 833-262-8899

Because of the dynamic nature of the Internet, any web addresses or links contained in this book may have changed
since publication and may no longer be valid. The views expressed in this work are solely those of the author and do
not necessarily reflect the views of the publisher, and the publisher hereby disclaims any responsibility for them.

Any people depicted in stock imagery provided by Getty Images are models,
and such images are being used for illustrative purposes only.
Certain stock imagery © Getty Images.

This book is printed on acid-free paper.

ISBN: 978-1-4520-2413-4 (sc)

Print information available on the last page.

Published by AuthorHouse 07/08/2022

authorHOUSE®

Little buddy was a small white bison poodle who loved to get into everything. He loved destroying the garbage and shedding paper all over the hall.

So, today was no different. As soon as he heard the door close, Buddy sprang into action.

First, he took a trip around the kitchen searching for any minute crumbs that just may be lying on the floor. No luck!

Then he ran to the living room. He jumped on his favorite sofa. You know the one with all the bright colors; pink, green, white, and blue. He especially loved the small wing chair in the corner with the big white pillow. It reminded him of his mom. It was also Ann's birthday gift from her sister!

He tried to pull some of the shiny hearts off of it because they looked like candy. Buddy tried and tried but he couldn't seem to get them a loose.

After taking a nap on his favorite chair, he went to the computer room. Ha! "Here's something," he thought to himself. "I wonder how this tastes," he pondered to himself. Let's see!

Buddy began to chew on the blue ink cartridge. It tastes kind of funny. As he chewed, more and more ink began to squirt out until Buddy was covered all over

with dark, smooth, blue ink. The more he rubbed his body with his little paws, the more he spread ink onto his once fluffy white coat. Until...Buddy wasn't a fluffy white poodle but a blue mess!

Although there were more things to get in to, Buddy began to feel not so good inside. He really didn't look good outside either. He felt sad and sick. He went to his bed and waited for his owners to return.

Usually Buddy would hear them and immediately run to the door to greet them, but not this time. When his masters, Willis and Ann came home, they shouted both at the same time, "Buddy, where are you?" Buddy didn't come out. They began to wonder what had happened; why he wasn't there. They began to look everywhere. He came down the stairs. Finally, with her eyes as wide as she could stretch them and her mouth opened, Ann shouted, "Oh no! Willis, come right away!"

They looked at each other in amazement. Willis shouted, "Buddy, what have you done? You've been a bad dog!" Buddy's little ears dropped and his sad eyes had water in them. He began to walk away slowly. Willis picked him up.

"Into the tub you go, you naughty dog!"

Willis scrubbed and scrubbed but Buddy was still blue.

The next afternoon, buddy had to go to the veterinarian.

He was given a shot and lots of medicine.

Next, Buddy had to go the groomer. Everyone laughed at the little blue dog in the window. Buddy wasn't blue anymore. He wasn't white anymore. Now he was PINK!!!! The groomer had to shave off all of Buddy's fluffy white hair!!!

After many weeks, Buddy began to feel better and his hair began to slowly grow back. First, it was a little fuzz. Then there was a little fluff. He looked like a little cotton ball with legs. When Willis would pick him up, he felt soft and cozy in his arms.

Soon Buddy was back to his happy little white fluffy self. But he decided from then on, he'd rather be white, fluffy and happy rather than have another "blue" day.

The End.

Printed in the United States
by Baker & Taylor Publisher Services